The
Medusa Mare

by
Charley Hendren

Copyright 1999 by:
The Cowboyography Corral,
P.O. Box 909, Douglas, WY 82633

Dedicated to my mother,
who first introduced me to the wonder
of tales fashioned in rhyme and meter.

Thank You's!

A special thanks goes to Miss Fronie. She is not only my wife but she is also my very best friend, my greatest supporter and my most honest critic. Without her, I'd surely be no good at all -

A deep "Thank you kindly!" to my good friend and poetry pard, Bo Bowman of Stillwater County, Montana, for the fine illustrations appearing herein. Bo, you penned what I could only see in my mind -

A "couldn't've done it without you!" to my friends Steve and Julie Bennett, who saddled up to guide me across the wild computer ranges -

A nod and heartfelt "muchas gracias!" to the real cowboys, the family ranchers, and the many westerners-of-the-heart who have kept the West alive -

And, finally, a humble thanks to my Lord and Savior for allowing me to live and write about the life I love so well.

Introduction

Looking back, it probably came as no surprise to my folks that their little boy wanted to be a cowhand when he grew up. After all, we lived just a few miles off the old Chisholm Trail on the plains of southern Kansas, and only one good day's ride from the historic cow town of Wichita. One might say I inherited my western affections honestly, for my daddy once cowboyed for pay on the King Ranch, my maternal great-grandpa Nichols was an honest-to-gosh old-time Texas trail drover, and my grandma's honeymoon consisted of three days spent on the trail in a covered wagon.

And while I've never been a surenuf, wage-earnin' cowhand by the stretch of anyone's imagination, it has been my great pleasure to live out West, ride big country with real hands, work cattle from the back of an honest horse, and apply the occasional branding iron.

Those experiences form the basis for many of the poems in this book. While not each poem reflects actual persons and events, a goodly number do bear a suspicious similarity to real people and situations, taken from the cow ranges of yesterday and today. In each, I've tried to stay true to the singular attitudes, lifestyles, philosophies and downright unique humor of those fortunates who call the West *Home*.

I've heard it said that the West is a state of mind as much as it is a place on a map. While sharing *the cowboy way* across the height and breadth of the U.S., I have found that to be a generally true statement, at least when it comes to the West of the heart. For reasons that I think I understand but cannot begin to express, a great many of us are drawn to the myth and the reality of the cowboy life, to visions of sweaty horses, campfires, creaking saddle leather, cattle bawl, and starry western skies.

It is with such visions in mind that I am downright tickled to offer these simple rhymes of the range to you. I hope they are true to the world they represent, and that they will bring a laugh, maybe a tear, and perhaps an occasional moment of reflection on how we all fit into the Good Lord's grand scheme of life. Wishing you a good ride!

Charley Hendren
The Circle-Double H Outfit,
Converse County, Wyoming, 1999

The Bill of Fare

As you head North from Casper, Wyoming on Interstate 25, you soon top out over a hill right at Mile Marker 215. From that point on a clear day, you can see the huge basin that forms what is known as the "Powder River Country" spread out before you, with the distant Bighorn Mountain Range creating a distant hazy blue horizon. It's an inspiring sight, and one that always serves to remind me how very much the Good Lord has blessed me to live in The Cowboy State.

Powder River Country

On the northern edge of Heaven, underneath the Western sky
There's a fair and handsome country,
And she's sittin' high and wide.

It's the Powder River country and she is somethin' to behold,
With endless hills and valleys
And water clear and cold.

She's a cowman's Paradise, with grass all growin' tall,
And snowmelt cricks runnin' clear
From Spring clear into Fall.

She can feed the cows that feed the world if treated with respect,
And raise the finest horses, boys,
The best you'll ever sit.

2

Lookin' to her North, risin' from the land
Sit the mountains named for wolves
Near Custer's final stand.

Viewin' to the East, the land rolls on and on
To the middle of Tomorrow
And the Black Hills siren song.

Checkin' to the South the country stretches out
Toward that outlaw hideout called
The Hole within the Wall.

And buildin' in the West there sits the Bighorn Range,
And a fairer batch of mountains
The Good Lord never made.

She's stood the test of Father Time and looked on through the years
Watchin' as the mountain men
Made their journeys here.

She's watched the first Americans fight their losin' fight,
And heard the cowboy singin'
To his cattle in the night.

She's seen the settlers leave their mark and cultivate her hills;
Seen the stretchin' of the wire
Dividin' up her spoils.

Through the years she's held her own with all that's come her way;
She's been a friend to them she trusts
And she's sent the rest away.

'O, she's got her moods and temper, her drought and winter freeze,
But if you'll take her on her terms
She'll meet your ever' need.

And she's waitin' there right now, if you think you've got the try
To be a part of all she is
And you'll vow to treat her right.

So if you'd dare, come. Saddle up. And strike with me a lope
To my Powder River country
And the ranges I call home.

They say that truth is stranger than fiction, and "Charlie and the Calumet Can" offers living proof of it. While I was not present when the "calumet can calamity" took place, I have it on good cowboy authority that it did indeed happen. When my friend R. W. Hampton shared this tale with me a few years ago, I knew immediately that I just HAD to reduce it to writing!

Charlie and the Calumet Can

In the far southwestern corner of our nations' 'Cowboy State',
The ranchin' folks still shake their heads at the cruel, ignoble fate
Of a pardner true, an honest friend, a son born of the land,
And they still lament the tearful tale of Charlie and the Calumet can.

Now Charlie was a cowman bold, bred to the western plains.
A surenuf hand, he built a spread on the high Red Desert range.
Fer sixty years he buckaroo'd thru heat and cold and wind -
Helped the neighbors, sang in church, and proved hisself a friend.

All was well in Charlie's world the year he met his end;
His lovin' wife and kids were fine and the cattle gathered in.
The shippin' that October brang prices record high;
The bank was paid, the pantry stocked and the winter hay laid by.

But came that sad and fateful day, a Monday I recall,
When Charlie woke up feelin' poor with a naggin' sorta cough.
He cowboyed up and made the day but as that evenin' fell
He told his wife and children, "I ain't feelin' very well".

Charlie worsened through the night. With the comin' dawn
His lovin' family learned the worst - their mate and dad was gone.
The word spread quickly round about - a beloved pard was dead;
"He's rode acrost that Great Divide" is what the neighbors said.

The funeral service was the best; the choir sang saintly songs
Whilst the preacher spoke a eulogy to the tightly gathered throng.
It woulda been near perfect if not for one slight hitch:
The weather turned off chilly; a Norther had blown in

And left the crick banks thick with ice, the sage with silver hue;
The temperature had plummeted to **minus forty-two!**
And therein lay the problem - the ground was froze up hard;
There weren't no way to dig a grave to lay away their pard!

But Charlie's lovin' widow, she pondered for a bit
On how they might just overcome this *snag* that they had hit.
She said, "Folks, you know my Charlie loved this desert range.
He loved to watch the cattle grazin' on the plains,

And I recall that he once said, 'When comes my final rest,
I don't want no casket lid to press upon my chest.
I'd ruther be cremated, my ashes freely spread
To drift across my desert range here in the open West'."

So Charlie was cremated and poured into a vase,
The ashes sent home with his wife to wait a sunny day;
To wait the comin' of the Spring when all the world was green
To loft dear Charlie's ashes upon some gentle breeze.

But then, by chance, that vase did *c-r-a-c-k* one cold and bitter day.
Charlie's wife grew sore afraid that he might blow away,
So quick she thought and quick she moved to save her precious man;
She dumped her Charlie's ashes in a bakin' powder can.

O'course the can was empty, its contents long removed,
Used to build the finest biscuits that ere met a tooth.
The can was labeled *"Calumet - The Finest in the Land"*,
And there she moved and there she left the remnants of her man.

So Charlie's ashes took their ease till Spring came once again,
Put back on a pantry shelf secure from seekin' hands,
Secure from winter's frigid blast, secure from cold and ice,
Securely placed till Spring erased the chill of winter's bite.

Now with the endin' of the cold the ranch returned to life,
With preparations underway for brandin' and the like.
The roundup wagon wheels was greased, the harness cleaned and oiled,
The horses brought in off the range with buckin' contests held.

The cowboys rolled their soogans and buckled on their chinks,
Set each trusty felt on square and tightened up each cinch.
They tied their slickers on behind, stepped aboard their mounts,
Moved in behind the wagon and smartly headed out

To do their cowboy duty out on the open range
Where they would stay thruout the Spring, performin' puncher things.
It made a Charlie Russell scene and the boys was feelin' gay
Except for when they pondered on poor Charlie laid away.

Each buckaroo recalled a tale of Charlie in his prime,
And each remembered Charlie's ways. "Why I recall one time,"
Some hand would start, and all would cock an ear
To hear of Charlie on the range in other, younger years;

Like when he roped that bobcat and put him on the fight;
He got that feline so durn mad he clum up Charlie's line!
Or when he broke his leg that day when fallin' with his horse,
And how he built a topnotch spread with nerve and honest work.

Four weeks passed. The crew was camped beside a purlin' crick;
The work was done and all relaxed while evenin' chuck was fixed.
The sun was low, the sky was clear, and the boys was restin' back
When Cookie said, "I've got bad news; there'll be no bread tonight,

Fer I'm fresh out of fixin's with which to knead and roll
My bakin' powder biscuits that yew fellers all love so.
I'm shore sorry, boys. Shoulda brang more Calumet,
But she's all gone so beans and beef is what yew'll only get."

Well, the boys all sat and pondered on what they'd heard him say.
No bakin' powder biscuits? That weren't the *cowboy* way!
The silence grew till it was loud. Then RW cleared his throat;
"I thought I saw an extry can behind them mixin' bowls."

Cookie said, "I'll take a look and purely hope yer right,
And if yew are I'll build a batch of biscuits worth yer time."
So Cookie checked the kitchen box and rustled 'mongst the pans.
"Here she is! More Calumet! Boys, this here is grand!"

And in no little time at all the crew was eatin' swell,
With biscuits light and pipin' hot and beefsteak done up well.
But as they sat back happy, RW spoke again;
"Boys, I'm not fer sure but lookin' at that tin

Of Calumet that Cookie found? Well, I'm sorta worried some.
Ain't that a 'X' scratched on the side? And ain't it like the one
That Charlie's widow marked that day last winter when she took
Ol' Charlie's ashes from that vase? Here boys, you take a look."

The crew all gathered 'round the can and ciphered out that 'X';
Sure enuff it looked the same. RW drew a breath.
"Now boys, I mean no disrespect. Ol' Charlie was the best,
And I loved him like a brother as you all will attest,

But maybe what we got here ain't really all that bad.
Charlie always told us how he loved this open land,
And I recall his missus said that day we bid adios
That Charlie wished his ashes *s-p-r-e-a-d* on the ranges he loved so.

Now the way I got it figgered, his wish has done come true -
He's still ridin' with the wagon and he's dang shore part of the crew!
And of all the things he ever done, now don't this take the cake?
Charlie makes the best durn biscuits I b'lieve I ever ate."

Have you ever known someone who was r-e-a-l good at always telling you the very best way to get anything and everything done just right, but somehow didn't get a whole lot accomplished on their own hook? I thought so. Well, it happens in the cowboy world, too, as the "Cowboy's Guide to Advice" illustrates.

The Cowboys' Guide to Advice

Advice is such a handy tool for those who hand it out,
With counsel kindly offered to them who are in doubt
Regardin' Life's rough, rocky road and trials that come their way,
And how to keep from stumblin' 'mongst the boulders ever' day.

Not only is it handy but the price is surely fine,
For friends who give **ADVICE**-ment never charge a dime.
They share their learn-ed wisdom just to be a pard,
To help a pal to cipher out some problem loomin' hard.

Like when you sit and ponder on the buyin' of a bull;
Will he prove a steady winner or be a useless cull?
Now **ADVICE** comes to the rescue: *"I'd just go ahead an' spend,
An' if yer cows are calfless? Well, yew'll have yer answer then."*

Or when you're sortin' pairs and you're down to just a few,
And they refuse to mother up and you're out of what to do:
*"Just throw that bunch of bawlin' calves into another pen
An' shut their mom's outside the gate - I'll bet they'll want 'em then."*

Or when you're at a ropin' and your luck is runnin' thin,
And you've just missed another loop and it's gettin' tough to grin:
*"Y'know, if yew would practice more, an' draw a slower steer,
An' keep that elbow tucked in close yew might just place - next year."*

12

Or you're out there in the round pen workin' with a colt,
And he has flang you all around and bit and tried to bolt.
ADVICE peers through the fence rails: *"I think yew've got 'im now.*
He has used yew an' abused yew till I think yew've wore him out."

Or you are at a brandin' and you've stretched your calf out neat,
But the feller with the brandin' iron *s-l-i-p-s* and nails your seat.
Never fear, **ADVICE** is here to soothe your wounded *pride*:
"Cowboy up - it ain't so bad - he mighta had the knife!"

Yep, **ADVICE** is fine and dandy and those who give it grand,
With words of cowboy wisdom across the western lands.
But I allow that most of them that offer helpful hints
Are seldom doin' anything 'cept leanin' on the fence.

Although line camps are relatively uncommon these days, there was once a time not so long ago when every sizable ranch had at least one. Stocked up with provisions and a string of horses, one or more cowboys would winter up in these camps, spending several frigid months chopping ice, turning back drifting cattle, and generally keeping an eye on the boss's bovine interests. For some it made for mighty lonely duty, but for others the "Line Camp" was a time to reflect and renew.

Line Camp

It's February - the time of year when Winter's lyin' deep.
Frost opaque's the windowpane and water's frozen in the crick.
All his books've been read once, with a few thumbed twice or more.
He sits with mended tack in hand and gazes t'ward the door.

These line camp days are wearin' thin, just like he knew they would
From all the camps he's been before when Winter spread its hood.
He's all alone unless you count the hosses in the shed
Munchin' hay he forked today, and the Good Lord overhead.

Sittin' there, his gaze expands and reaches past the door
Where right outside he sees the sky with a million stars or more.
And bidin' 'neath their silver light he views the mighty line
Of the Bighorn Range reachin' up in a postcard sorta night.

In his mind the snow is gone and the hills are hazy green,
  And in the place of cabin smoke he smells a newborn Spring.
  And rather than the cold that sneaks and crawls inside his vest,
  A gentle breeze trots easy by, makin' meadow grasses dance.

  From this reachin' reverie he concludes that all is well,
  For seasons last just for a time, much like this last cold spell.
  He reckons he can last one more, so let Winter now be king;
  Right outside that cabin door there waits another Spring.

Chuck Wagon Etiquette

RD an' me rode into camp
As Cookie was handin' out chuck.
We'd been in the saddle since just after dawn
An' was both feelin' sorter used up.

We curried the horses an' turned 'em on out,
Then stepped to the fire for a plate
An' got us a helpin' of biscuits an' beef
An' settled back on our bedrolls to eat.

16

Now all waddies know of the cardinal rule
Relatin' to cowboy chuck;
That no matter how *ruint* or *tasteless* or *foul*,
You just natcherly grin an' eat up.

While the rule is unspoken, it's known far an' wide
An' the puncher who breaks it may find
That he's now the cook, or maybe's been fired
While the rest of the crew ropes an' rides.

Knowin' full well this unwritten law,
I sorter raised up a brow in surprise
When Toby, the kid, speaks up an' says,
"These here biskits ain't tastin' quite right."

Well, a hush sorter settled down over the scene.
Ever' man's eye snuck a look
In the gen'ral direction of the pots an' the pans
An' the figure of Big Jim the cook.

Now Jim weren't real blessed with no lofty I.Q.
But there weren't nothin' wrong with his ears,
An' the instant that Toby's remark tumbled out
Jim's eyes started formin' a glare.

RD an' me? We kept on eatin'
Like our biskits was tastin' just fine
While Jim wiped his hands an' shucked off his apron
An' muttered a few words unkind.

Toby, he turns as pale as a ghost
When Jim takes this gonch hook in hand
An' fingers it easy an' checks out its length
With a look to turn glass back to sand!

Then Jim steps on acrost to the kid
An' he says in this dangerous tone,
"I don't guess that I heared you real well . . .
Is there somethin' you'd like me to know?"

So the stage was all set for a turrible wreck
Unless the kid could recover,
An' you could tell from his eyes he'uz studyin' real hard
On just how to survive this encounter!

Well, Toby ponders his plate and considers his fate
An' examines a biskit in hand.
Then he makes up his mind an' takes a deep breath
An' says, "Jim, you just don't understand."

Then he grins sorter hopeful an' states his defense.
"Jim, these here biskits is rank.
Why they're burned on the bottom an' raw on the top
An' as salty as any I've ate.

"Fact of the matter, I've only onct met
A biskit this sloppily built;
Your dough is shore lumpy an' your starter's so poor
It's a wonder we all ain't bin kilt."

An' my jaw drops a foot as the kid rambles on;
Says them biskits are "as hard as a rock".
The kid must be s-l-o-w or maybe insane
To engage in such dangerous talk.

If this is the plan to save his young skin
An' guarantee he'll survive,
If this defense is all he can mount,
He ain't gonna come out alive!

An' Toby don't quit! He warms to his task
An' describes the "sorry condition"
Of each biskit's form, whilst RD an' me
Cain't hardly believe what we're hearin'!

But I finally catch on as Toby concludes,
As he says in a voice smooth as butter,
"Yessir, these biskits remind me of home,
An' I'd shore like to have me another!"

Any true horseperson can recall at least one equine friend whose personality and traits caused him or her to stand out from the rest of the herd. The "Old Paint Mare" is one of them.

The Old Paint Mare

Tired she stood, all spraddled out;
There weren't much left to see.
Her head hung low and her ribs all showed;
She'd clearly gone to seed.

Ma and me, we stood nearby
And waited for the vet.
"It's best," we said, "to put her down;
Ol' Dream has reached the end."

Ma shed some tears while I hid mine
And bravely tried to act
Like, "After all, she's just a horse,
And we've got other mares out back."

But as we waited I must confess
That my memory began to run.
It took me back to years gone by
And all Ol' Dream had done.

Thirteen foals that mare had borne,
With every one a hit,
And every one a painty horse,
And most with blue-eyed squint.

A solid sixteen hands she stood,
A roany, red paint mare;
The pride of the Circle 2H place
And tophand winner there.

She'd shown her speed out on the track,
But could walk the trails true;
Had taught at least ten kids to ride
And a couple of grownups, too.

I recalled how she would ease along,
Just goin' with the flow,
But when your heels caressed her flanks,
You'd best be set to go!

My mind still saw her strong and proud;
My ears still heard the beat
From muscled legs in easy lope
When in her prime she'd been.

Then we heard a pick-up truck -
The vet had just arrived.
Ma turned to me and whispered,
"I've got to go inside."

I nodded, for I understood
What Ma was feelin' deep.
I dreaded what was comin'
As Dream was put to sleep.

But she had stuck through thick and thin,
Through colts and colic, too,
And after all she'd done for us
'Twas the least that I could do.

Once the vet had done the deed
I stepped off all alone,
Out beyond those 2H stalls
That Dream had known as home.

I stood awhile, just rememberin'.
Then I looked up to the sky
And whispered, "Lord, You've got her now
And I know You'll treat her right.

"She a stubborn sort and tough to catch,
But don't You never mind;
That old paint mare will do You proud
And I thank You for her time.

"And Lord, it is a comfort to my soul
To know she's grazin' up on high,
While I wait the day we'll saddle up,
That old paint mare and I."

I am mighty proud of the fact that my dad cowboyed for the famous King Ranch in Texas. Much more importantly, though, I am proud and grateful that he took the time to teach me how to live like I ought. Thanks, Dad!

Father's Day Letter

Dear Dad, I sit to write and trust you're doing fine.
You know how Spring is at the ranch; it's hard to find the time
To pen a note, but here I am and I hope this finds you well.
Branding's done, the grass is up, and we should do all right come Fall.

Branding chores took me back to when I was a kid, and
How I sure looked up to you, watching all you did.
Remember all the time you took to teach me how to rope?
Kidding me when I would miss but never losing hope?

Dad, it's mighty strange the things I value now
That once I took for granted, like the way you taught me how
To handle newborn foals and recognize their needs,
Or how to work a spooky colt when teaching him to lead,

And how a momma cow brute will hide her newborn calf, and
Where to look and where she'll be four times out of five.
Or how to watch the skyline and know if there'll be rain
Before the dawn or if the weather'll likely stay the same.

But that's not all. You also showed me how to be a man,
To take a stand and to count for good and do the best I can.
The boots you filled not many men would even try for fit,
And you taught me that the boots I wear leave tracks of who I am.

Looking back, I learned a lot from schooling in your class,
With lessons taught and daily tests that I both failed and passed.
I know I took for granted the way you brought me on;
It didn't mean a nickel then, but now I understand.

Your two grand kids sure make a pair, not knowing 'yes' from 'can't'!
If I was much like them at all, you must have wanted bad
To turn me out from time to time and just let me go my way.
Dad, I'm glad you held on to the lead is what I want to say.

I guess it's sorta lonely with Mom gone now a year,
And I've been lately thinking that you should be out here
Instead of living in that box they call a house in town.
The wife and kids would love it, and Dad I'd sure be proud.

Well, I guess that's pretty much all I had to say.
There's fence to ride and other chores and I'd better face the day.
Dad, I hope you will consider this last I wrote about.
Call me, please, and let me know. I could come and bring you out.

P.S. I've cleaned up your old saddle – that Wade you like to sit;
She's clean and oiled and ready for a few more gathers yet.
Well, I really have to close. Dad, thanks for teaching me.
I'm thankful that
        You took the time
                And held on to the lead.

Your loving son.

There's always someone who wants "just one horse, or maybe a couple of 'em at most, to sorta keep around the place". But oftentimes it doesn't stop with just one. And then there's all the "stuff" that the horseperson needs in order to keep up with all the other horsepersons (or is it horsepeople?), and pretty soon you're wondering just who owns who. Needless to say, things can sure get out of hand in a hurry. If you see yourself in this poem, take comfort. You're not alone!

Daydreamin'

I looked across the pasture at our horses grazin' there;
A gelded bay, a blaze face colt and a skinny sorrel mare.
They weren't high dollar horses; two were outright free
And the last we'd traded for some hay - a downright frugal fee.

Plainly put, 'twas a sorry lot with no confirmation trail;
The mare displayed a roman nose and the colt had ate her tail.
The bay had eyes a bit too wide plus an evil, toothy grin;
Sickle-hocked and some drawed up, he looked like equine sin.

That colt would never win a show, as anyone could see;
He had himself a gotched-up ear and matchin' gotched-up knees.
Sure as death, among these three not one would bring a nod.
I sighed and started dreamin' of some registration blood.

I dreamt I had me somethin' *nice* - a handsome band of steeds;
Horses papered thru and thru, with looks and moves to please.
I saw it all - me ridin' high, a king of all surveyed,
Wheelin' and dealin' with the best on expert deals parlayed.

But then I recollected some horsemen I had known
Who had such fancy, blooded stock they couldn't swing a loan;
Of insured cost to cut the loss if one should break a leg,
And of custom fence and heater vents and rubber-matted beds;

Of ropin' kacks and cuttin' chaps and halter showin' gear,
And air-conditioned outfits to move 'em there to here;
Of special grains and weedless hay to keep 'em in their prime,
With vitamins and special creams to cause their coats to shine;

Not to mention trainer fees to keep 'em at their best,
And English pants and fancy hats to wear for each event;
Of blankets for the winter and fans for summer heat, and
On and on my dreamin' went till a *nightmare* I could see!

Then I blinked and looked across that pasture once again
To view our sorry little band a'dozin' in the sun.
I slowly turned away and found I had to smile, for
I'd smartly reconsidered - they'ud do yet . . . for awhile.

There's a lot of happenings in this old world that seem beyond explanation, and this tale describes one of them. Not that I'm biased, but I will admit that "The Stranger" being one of my personal favorites.

The Stranger

RD and me leaned on the truck
Out front of *The Stockman's Café*.
We'd come into town to pick up supplies
And had turned it into a day.

> We'd said all our howdies to them that we knew
> And were purty much ready to go
> When out of the door of Frank's saddle store
> Stepped an old man - a stranger for sure.

28

I glanced at him close, but he just didn't fit.
I wondered where was he from. And that outfit he wore?
It wasn't made anymore
Leastways anywhere's that I'd been.

RD said, "Howdy, old dad; Are you new in these parts?
I guess I ain't seen you around."
He looked at us long, then quietly answered,
"I don't often make it to towns."

Then he turned for to go with his spurs softly jinglin',
Till I asked if he needed a lift.
He looked once again, then sighed and replied
That he figgered that maybe he did.

So we left out of town, headed back t'wards the ranch
And had gone prob'ly eight or ten miles
When the stranger pointed a thick, weathered finger
At a ruin way off in the sage.

"Got my first job at Old Man McCann's
When I was still too young to shave.
Lordy," he said, "I remember McCann
The day he got laid in his grave."

RD and me, we looked at each other,
Unsure of just how to reply.
Oh, we'd heard of McCann since we was both kids
And how he'd settled back in Seventy-Nine.

But the shiver that started at the base of my spine
And trickled on up 'cross my neck
Was caused by the knowin' that the year of his goin'
Was *Eighteen* and Seventy-Nine!

Nobody said nothin' fer a couple more miles;
I wondered if I'd heard him right.
Along about then the left front tire blew
With nary a spare in the rack.

We checked out the tire and she was a goner -
Had a two-fisted hole in the side.
It looked like we'd spend the night by the pickup
'Lessin' some neighbor chanced by.

And night was comin' so we built us a fire
Along of a streambed nearby.
We checked out the truck and found us some chuck -
A few cookies and crackers left by.

By the time it was dark we had us a camp,
Sittin' cross-legged around.
The wind in the sage and the fire's yellow blaze
Made a timeless sort of surround.

From under my hat I surveyed the stranger,
Who had not since offered a sound.
From the lines 'round his eyes it was easily surmised
That he'd ridden a trail hard and long.

I wanted to ask him where was he headed,
Tho' etiquette dictated silence.
But I wanted to ask and call him to task
When he pushed back his hat and he stated,

"Boys, I'm reminded of s'many campfires,
Sittin' by this one tonight;
Fires at the wagon when the herd was all gathered,
With stars just like these shinin' bright.

"All of my pards are gone now," he said;
"Angel, and Shorty, and Fred.
Angel got trampled one night in a storm'
An' Shorty got drown'd at the Red.

"Fred rode his last on a bronc we called Skippy;
A pony as high-strung as they come."
The old stranger nodded, recallin' his friends,
Then shook his head and went on

To tell us of grass belly deep to a horse,
Of a land unfettered by fence;
Of cattle pure mean and of water pure clean -
Why, he was History in old duckin' pants.

The old man spoke of Montana winters
With snow fallin' clear into June,
And of Mexican summers that lasted forever,
And of all the good horses he'd knew.

He spoke of trailin' the big herds up North,
Runnin' two and three-thousand head;
Of cowboys from Texas to the northernmost stretches,
And you could tell he had lived all he said.

RD and me? We sat there in silence,
Just hangin' on every word.
I felt olden times 'round the campfire that night;
The stranger had rolled back the years.

It must have been One or Two in the mornin'
When he pulled his hat down again.
I sure didn't git it but was glad that I'd heard it -
Them long ago days that had been.

The sun comin' up roused me from slumber.
When I looked, the stranger was *gone*!
I got up RD to have a look-see
But the old man'd disappeared with the dawn.

> We checked all around, past the stream and beyond,
> But found not even a track.
> I started to think that I'd dreamt the whole thing
> When RD called out from the truck.

That bad tire? It was perfect! No sign of a hole!
The flat might never have been!
RD and me, we looked at each other -
Was the stranger only imagined?

> Well, we scattered our ashes and made for to leave,
> Still glancin' around if by chance
> The old man had gone off by hisself
> And maybe would come back again.

But when we started the pick-up, my ear heard a jingle
From under the seat by the door.
I will never forget what I saw when I looked -
On the floor lay a *mexican spur*!

> There is no explanation I know of to tell
> What happened with RD and me.
> But happen it did and that spur by my bed
> Is all the proof that I need.

I think of the stranger ever' now and again;
How he moved in and out of our lives.
And wherever he is, I sure hope it's with friends
'Round an old-fashioned campfire tonight.

Take care Stranger, and stay clear of the wire.

No self-respecting cowboy wants to get caught pulling some fool stunt that might lead others to believe he is less than a Top Hand. And when such aforementioned stunt inevitably occurs, some will do almost anything but out-and-out lie in order to cover their embarrassed tracks. But, like the feller said, "the truth will out".

A True Ranch Story (or)
How I really Broke My Foot

The next thing I knew I was spread belly-up.
Ma brought the pick-up around
And helped me load in, then propped up my leg
And off we headed for town.

The Doc said, "Pardner, you've done it this time -
That foot is broke in three places!
I'll build you a cast and send you on home
But you aren't gonna be in no races

For ten or twelve weeks with those bones on the mend.
Now just how did you say this occurred?"
I just muttered, "I don't rightly recall,"
And had Ma get me out of there.

All the way home I considered my plight.
I'd shore be embarrassed to say
How that appendage *really* got broke
'Cause it shore weren't the 'cowboy way'.

Back at the ranch Ma fixed me up good,
But I was dreadin' the end of the day
When the boys would ride in and look at my foot
And ask what had happened to me.

34

And when evenin' arrived it was worse than I'd feared;
The whole dang crew traipsed right in
And examined my toes sittin' there on display
And asked of what wreck I'd been in.

But . . . all afternoon I'd been a'thinkin'
On how that foot *coulda* broke,
And I'd built me a story that I figgered would do, so
Humbly I let it unfold.

"Fellers, I know you're all anxious to hear
How I come to be laid up like this.
Now gather around and I'll tell you the tale
As best I remember it.

"I was out in the round pen, schoolin' that colt
That the Boss acquired from Ol' Donneley,
But just when I thought the lesson was done,
He rare'd up and then *stomped* on me soundly!"

Now I figgered the boys would easy buy that.
(Heck, I nearly believed it m'self!)
But they just stood there not sayin' a word,
So real quick I tried somethin' else.

"Oh . . . yeah . . . now I recall - I was workin' the bay
And checkin' his manners and such
When he ran through the bit and caught my poor foot
Between of his ribs and the fence."

Well, I glanced at the boys to see how that took.
They just stood there with thumbs hooked in jeans . . .
And waited . . . just . . . waited. I started to sweat,
Tryin' to conjure up a good scene.

"Uh . . . hmmm . . . that weren't it neither but she's comin' back now!
I was just fixin' to mount up the . . . uh . . . the dun,
When he sidestepped and kicked and threw such a fit
That he caught me right square on the foot."

The boys only blinked and looked at the floor.
I could tell at a glance I was done.
I'd rode with this crew and they knew me too well,
So I sighed and I grinned and 'fessed up.

"Boys," I said, "I'm ashamed to admit
How I broke this here foot late this morn',
But you boys are my pards so I've got to come clean -
I tripped . . . comin' outta . . . the john . . ."

We can all look back on trails taken that changed the course of our lives and afforded us new and exciting experiences that the years slowly turned to memories.
But no matter the chosen trail, there always remain other memories from other trails, each to be taken out, dusted off, and fondly recalled from time to time

Lovin' From Afar

In the chill September evenin'
When the autumn breeze comes creepin'
 And the coffee on the fire is bubblin' low,

It's then his mind'll wander
To years long past and yonder
 To a special gal he left so long ago.

He'll sit there in the quiet,
 Gazin' t'ward the distant high-ups
 And wonder how she's been and where she lives,

And one more time he'll ask
 What might've come to pass
 If he'd but had the nerve to make her his.

O', it ain't that she weren't special,
 With her smile and eyes of hazel,
 Or that she wasn't fine to be around.

It's just that distant ranges
 And the smell of trampled sages
 Won his heart o'er security and towns.

So in the chill of evenin'
 When thoughts of *her* come creepin'
  Midst campfire glow and evenin' prairie stars,

Knowin' that the cowboy way
 Is how he'll always earn his pay,
  He's content to love her memory - from afar.

> *If you have ever visited a ghost town, you know what it is like*
> *to stand in its dusty street or on one of its decayed boardwalks*
> *and picture what it must have been like way back when.*

The Nameless Town

This nameless town is silent now. It's been that way for years,
Ever since the railroad left midst steam and oily gears.

Those restless souls who came so bold to make a town-site grow
Moved off to follow newer tracks some hundred years ago

And left their dream a lonely scene, the only street o'ergrown
With prairie grass and dusty sage, the faded buildings blown

By wind and rain and wind again, left to sag and sway;
Weathered temples to the hopes of those who moved away.

Now tourists from the cities come in rented vans and jeeps,
Searching for the West of old, a West their spirits seek.

Here they'll snap their photographs while striking outlaw pose,
Leaning near the barroom door or at a boardwalk post.

And then they're gone. Once again the nameless town grows still,
Except upon the evening breeze a shift of time is felt.

Upon the breeze piano keys strike up an ancient tune
While lights appear in windows that moments past were gloom.

And boot steps sound. They gently pound along the boarded walk,
Above the turn of wagon wheel and quiet evening talk.

Trace chains jingle, mix and mingle with the phantom sounds,
Adding meter to the scene as western sun goes down.

Unheard laughter, silent banter rises with the moon,
Timeless echoes from the past when once the town was new.

This nameless town is living now, its past a present thing
When ranchers, miners, settlers came to build their secret dreams.

Then shots ring out, with hollow shouts echoing the ring,
Followed close by running sounds, fleeing from the scene

As hoof beats pound and loud resound along the empty street;
An unseen killer gallops by once more bent on escape.

All those hopes and dreams and schemes wait just beyond the day,
Rising with the purple glow of sundown's final ray, till

With the dawn there comes a yawn. The nameless town grows still,
Resting back in dusty sleep to wait the daily mill

Of tourists from the cities come in rented vans and jeeps,
Searching for the West of old -

A West their spirits seek.

Among the many traits that tend to set cowboys apart from other folks, one has to be their most unique sense of humor. But sometimes, as in "The Makin's of a Hand", the object of the humor ends up having the last laugh.

Many people have asked me if this is a true story. Well, I guess you'll just have to decide for yourself.

The Makin's of a Hand

"**Come** by 'round five next Friday,"
Ma said as we left church.
"We'll have a bite of supper
And show you 'round the place."

       "Maa-velous," said Mrs. Hensley.
       Replied her husband Theodore,
       "You know we're lately of the city.
       We've never seen a ranch before."

They couldn't wait to see the outfit,
With our 'daaa-ling little calves'.
They couldn't wait to pet the horses,
So 'honest, pure, and proud'.

42

Well, I scratched out some directions
To help 'em find their way.
I gave Theodore our number
But then I had to say,

"Now folks, a ranch is a workin' place
So you might best come prepared.
Wear old jeans, nothin' fancy now,
'Cause things gets used out there."

"Yes, yes, of course,"
Came back his cit-tee-fied reply;
"We both have hats and boots
And I am sure they will suffice."

"Well I'm just shore they will",
I muttered as I slightly rolled my eyes,
Thinkin' *Ma, what have you gone*
*And done to us **this** time?*

So the fateful Friday finally came
As I knew it had to do.
It'ud rained all week and the place was soaked
But at Five I heard the t-o-o-t

From the horn of a BMW
As the Hensley's splashed on in,
And I choose to call it fateful
'Cause the nightmare then began.

Them city slickers wore matchin' shirts
Of neon-es-ent *orange!*
I'd never in my whole borned life
Seen clothes like that before!

Their boots was new and neatly formed
Of full-quill ostrich skin
And I'ud bet my summer wages
They was hand built stern to stem.

I just sorter shook my head
As politely as I knew.
Ma asked 'em in but Miz Hensley said,
"Might we tour before we do?"

"Shore," I sighed, "But watch yer step -
It's a little (heh, heh) boggy over there."
But I'ud spoke too late! She'd disappeared!
Clean up to her hair!

Now Mr. Hensley was mighty game,
I gotta give 'im that;
He dove on in to save her
And he landed with a s-p-l-a-t,

And when they emerged, them fancy shirts
Weren't so neon anymore;
Fact was, all their clothes
Was sorter boggy to the core.

Ma toweled 'em off. I hoped they'ud leave
Cause I had work to do.
But n-o-o-o, they had to "see the stock",
So I decided to show 'em Blue.

Now Little Blue weren't nothin' much,
Just a gelded, mixed-blood grade;
Nine-hundred pounds and fourteen hands
Of pure satanic *HATE*!

See, Blue could not be trusted
From one second to the next.
He'd buck, or bite, and usually both;
Blue'ud get 'em off the place!

"Is he friendly?" asked Theodore
As he dripped against the rail.
Ma tried to speak but I said, "Well, shore!
Why, a child could pull his tail.

"Now pardner, this little pony
Would not harm a fly.
He's broke to death, a real puppy dog,
And (heh, heh) you can mount 'im either side.

"Fact is, I'll just catch 'im up
And you can try 'im out.
You can ride 'im in the co-rral
And sorter ease 'im round."

Now lookin' back, it weren't as funny
As I'ud envisioned at the time,
Tho' Blue, he stood kid-gentle
As the bridle I hung on.

He didn't even pin his ears
When Theodore stroked his nose,
And didn't twitch a muscle
When I said (heh, heh), "Up you go".

"*O', do be careful!*" shrilled Mrs. H.
As her hero crawled aboard.
And I'm convinced 'Twas her very shrill
That made Blue come pure *undone*!

Just as Mr. Hensley thought
He was settled up on top,
Blue, he kinder skittered
And then I heard a *pop!*

From the bridle Blue was wearin'
As it broke clean half in two
And off they took around the pen.
Well, (heh, heh) there weren't much *I* could do.

Now like I said, Mr. H. was game.
He was hangin' on fer life,
But ever' time his rear came down,
Ol' Blue's was aimin' high!

So round they went, up and down
And bouncin' end to side;
Mr. Hensley with white-knuckle grip
And Blue with stiff-legged stride.

This went on fer twelve laps 'round
And I allowed he'ud make the ride
Till Blue wore out. But then I saw
The gleam in the geldin's eye.

Blue had spied his water trough.
I swear I saw 'im grin.
He locked up all four wheels at once,
And Theodore? He shot right in!

He disappeared beneath the waves,
Then slowly reappeared.
With hat awash, he clambered out
And never said a word;

Just nodded sorter vacant-like
As I steered 'im from the pen;
Gave no sign of recognition
When Blue *bit* 'im just fer grins.

The couple limped back to their car
And quietly got in,
Her covered up with bog
And him in matching pen.

"Won't you stay for supper?"
Ma pleaded 'fore they left,
Glancing my direction
With a look of pending death.

"I'm sorry. We can't," came the reply
From bruised and battered chin.
"But we'd like to, soon," he added,
"Return and ride . . . again."

And I noticed he sat straighter.
And I saw a look of pride.
I beheld a sense of purpose
Behind his twin blacked eyes.

And as they drove away, I thought,
Now, inside that city skin
There's the makin's of a cowboy.
"Ma, I b'lieve he'll make a hand."

My great-grandpa Nichols was a Texas trail drover in the 1890's. Although he went on to his reward long before I came along, I think of him often and fondly.

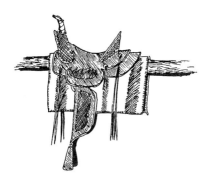

If I Had Rode With Grandpa

When I ride out on the mornin'
And I'm horseback 'cross the sage,
I'll sometimes get to thinkin'
On that near-forgotten age

When the ranges had no fences
And the trails weren't known as roads,
When the West was young and growin'
And there weren't no power poles.

That's how my grandpa saw it,
Pushin' Longhorns on the trail
From Texas up to Kansas
'Neath skies where eagles sailed.

He rode those ever-reachin' plains
On a string of mustang horses;
Saw the Comanche and the buffalo
And swam the river courses.

Grandpa Nichols earned his pay
From a Mother Hubbard saddle
While he looked at life a'horseback
Behind the Longhorn cattle.

He worked for forty and his found.
He slept beside the wagon
And he took his turn at nightguard
Underneath the stars of Heaven.

O', what a time that must have been
To ride the open range!
And to thank the Lord you done it
With the knowin' it would change.

For now the trails are mostly gone,
Except for highway signs
To mark the trails of ancient herds
That my Grandpa helped to drive.

And I will wonder if he ever thought
That he'd someday be an idol
To a world that often wishes
For trails and Longhorn cattle.

Now I know you can't stop progress;
  I know Life depends on change,
 And Grandpa's times are history now
Upon the yellowed page,

  But sometimes when I'm thinkin'
  On how it must have been,
 I'll find myself a'wishin'
That I had been with him

  And that we had rode together
  Out on some early morn
 When the ranges had no fences.
And the West was bein' born.

Even if you've never had the pleasure of riding a good horse out on big country, it's for sure that you've met someone very much like the central figure in the "The Complainer". I know I have.

The Complainer

Say there, pard, is that the campfire ahead?
I cain't hardly see, my eyes are so red
From fightin' the dust that we've ate all day long;
It seems like ferever since we mounted at dawn.

Could yew believe all them bunch quitters today?
With each one dead set to go the wrong way?
S'pecially that brockle with the crookedy horn;
T'ween her an' her calf, my rear's sorter worn.

An' how 'bout this weather? Near fifty this mornin',
But that Norther come in and it shore fixed to blowin'.
I cain't feel m'hands and m'feet's mostly froze,
An' it looks like it's prob'ly fixin' to snow.

I shore hope my bedroll is warmer tonite;
Got 'er wet in that drenchin' we had a while back
An' she ain't dried out since an' I hate to be cold;
Most likely a sign that I'm gettin' old.

Did yew see my jug-headed hoss at Fish Crick
When he tried to pitch me after takin' a drink?
An' he doggone near done it! I barely hung on.
He's the loco'dest hoss I guess I ever bin on!

Say, why cain't we git better hosses to ride?
This string that I'm on just beats my insides.
There's nary a one has got any sense
An' ever' day's ride is a Kodak event.

Dang, but I'm weary of ol' Cookie's chuck;
His beans an' his stew all taste like bad luck.
Good cooks *must* be out there, fer I've not met one worse;
It makes a man wonder if he's under a curse!

Do yew think the boss'll keep us on thru the winter?
I'm too broke to quit an' I'm too old to wander,
But the way he's bin talkin' 'bout profits an' loss
A feller don't know which way he might toss.

This cowboy lifestyle shore gits mighty mean,
What with weather, bad hosses an' wages so lean.
An' long days, an' chuck that'll twist yer insides;
Why, only a fool'ud hang in fer the ride!

I swear that I'm through! Gonna hang up my spurs
An' head me to town to sit out m'years.
I'm cut up on cattle! Yew can have all my share;
When we git back in, I'm a'leavin' for shore!

Gonna sign on where I kin prop up my feet,
Where the wages is good an' the duty is sweet,
Where the biskits is light an' the coffee ain't cold;
Yessirree, pard, I'm fixin' to fold.

But hold up now . . . is that the wagon up there?
An' there's all the boys, an' each one of 'em's square.
There's RD and John and that new feller, too;
All in all, they ain't such a bad crew.

Hey, an' look at the sky. Them clouds are a'breakin'.
Looks like we've got a nice night in the makin'.
There's the Big Dipper an' don't she look fine
Sittin' easy up there and markin' her time?

Boy, the smell of that coffee shore tickles my nose;
B'lieve I'll git me a cup and drink 'er down slow.
An' git a whiff of that chuck! I'm gonna grab me a plate
An' git wrapped 'round a bunch of them beans and that steak!

Yew know, a feller could do worse than to cowboy fer pay.
Not many left git to live this here way.
'Course some fellers complain 'bout the cowpuncher life,
But not me, yew kin bet . . . I like it right fine.

Honest, I have no earthly idea where "Klucker" came from. It just sorta happened one hot summer afternoon as I was driving across West Texas, headed from Forth Worth to El Paso. Maybe it was all those miles of nothing but miles.

Klucker the Kow Chickin

Now Klucker the kow chickin was a genuine pard
An' the very best cowboy I knew.
No matter the work or the ride to be made
Ol' Klucker would see the job through.

'Course some folks would laugh when they saw him an' me,
Ridin' together at saddle,
With me in the seat an' handlin' the reins
An' Klucker a'forkin' the cantle.

Klucker had him his very own hat,
A Resistol I'd had special tooled,
An' with the silken bandanner he wore 'round his neck
He provided a most memorable view.

But like I was sayin', Ol' Klucker was good;
That chickin could hang with the best.
Fact of the matter I never onct saw
A hand better suited fer brush.

See, Klucker would go where a hoss would not dare;
He'ud charge straight into mesquite
An' surprise them ol' cows a'hidin' in there,
All brushed up an' beatin' the heat.

He carried a rope coiled loose 'round his neck,
Slung high since he weren't too tall.
He'd shake out a loop with his sun-weathered beak
An' twirl 'er around an' let sail.

Well them cows? They never figgered on such from a *chickin*!
They'd just look an' ignore an' go on
'Til Klucker would dab him a horn or a hoof
An' then dally his end on a rock.

An' fer trailin' a bunch? He had not the equal.
No one could even come close.
Any fool cow even thinkin' to stray
Could expect a sharp peck on the nose!

An' evenin's in camp when the work was all done,
He'd sit with the crew 'round the fire;
We'd sing while he'd kluck the old cowboy songs
Till time to turn in fer the night.

'Twas a hot August day I shall never forget,
When Klucker made his last ride.
We'uz up on the Sandy a'lookin' fer strays
An' turnin' the ones we could find

When Klucker give out with his *There's a kow!* kluck.
Well, I turns in the saddle to see
This big brindle bull standin' alone
'Neath a pin oak, a'hidin' from me.

Klucker dismounted an' started his run,
Headed fer the big brindle's nose.
Just like he'd done all durin' the day,
He'ud turn this last one fer home.

But that bull was a killer, as I see clearly now;
He waited fer my pardner to close,
Then hooked with his horn in the blink of an eye
As Klucker jumped up fer his nose!

'Twas sad but 'Twas true; my pardner was gone.
The bull's deadly horn found its target.
I still sorta shudder rememberin' the scene
That hot August day Klucker bought it.

But if in my grief there is some consolation,
It's the good times I still can recall
Ever' time I see Klucker,
      Fer I brung him back home

           An' had 'im stuffed

           An' that's him

              Over there

                On the wall.

It is rather surprising to me that women are among the most unsung heroes of the West. After all, the cowboy life may be one of the least sexist occupations in all of history. And it's for sure that cows and the ranges they graze couldn't care less about the gender of the hand who's doing the work.

I hope the story of the "Ranch Woman" honors all female cowboys and women of the West.

Ranch Woman

She came to the West as a blushing young bride,
Leaving the big urban sprawl
To follow his dream of horses and cattle,
And hearing the coy-o-tee call.

She said she would go, recalling her vows
To honor and love and obey,
Though she's never been West or worked on a ranch
And she didn't know cheatgrass from hay.

But he had some money from when his dad died
And he figured with that they could start,
So they bought them a place through a magazine deal
And got a used truck and came on.

Now the property deed said the ranch had a stream
And some twelve-odd sections in fence,
But on their arrival the streambed was dry
And the fence barely held up itself.

And the ranch house was sadly in need of repair,
But she knew it would just have to do;
She could tell from the light in her young husband's eyes
He was home. So she was home, too.

"It'll be fine," he promised the girl
Who stood by his side at their gate.
"It'll take time but I know it'll work.
You'll see. This place'll be great."

So she set up housekeepin' as good as she might;
They bought 'em some stock and made friends
With the neighborin' ranchers who lived roundabout
And who helped 'em to get settled in.

That first year was tough, learnin' the work
And makin' that old ranch house do;
She put up some curtains from bedsheets they had
And planted a flower or two.

And she also learned cattle from the back of a horse –
How to ride and to dally a rope,
And sometimes she cried, exhausted at night,
But she never let on to her beau.

Things were still tough in years two and three
And some months they barely hung on.
Still, through it all, they worked and they learned
And she knew it was here they belonged.

By now there was a baby to care for and love,
And the neighbors said many's the time
They watched Mom drag calves to a hot brandin' fire
With the little boy perched on behind.

When their little girl came, she stayed more to home,
Not workin' the ranges so much.
'Course by now she could rope and catch her own horse
And still manage to keep the place up.

Her figure was still the same through it all,
Though the lifestyle had weathered her skin;
There were lines 'neath her brow from fightin' the sun
But it didn't matter because

Her husband still called her the prettiest gal
That he guessed he had ever laid eyes on;
He still held her hand at the end of the day
And he still kissed her face ever' morn.

Well the poets have said that time marches on,
That it waits for no man. Or woman.
And so it was true for these city-born two
Who aged with the ranch they'd begun.

The kids grew. The boy left but the daughter stayed on
For it seemed she was born to the life.
Her momma had taught her how to ride and to cook
And how to hay and to sew and the like.

So as years galloped by, as years tend to do,
The bride from the East came to know
A love and respect for the life that was hers,
With a peace carried deep in her soul.

With the soft April rain of their fifty-ninth Spring
Since comin' to the West that she loved,
The ranch woman lay 'neath a quilt she had made
And heard angels in chorus above.

The kids were both there, as was her man
Who sat quiet with his hand on hers
And patted it gentle, like a filly just born,
And silently blinked back the tears.

She looked at them all, then struck up a smile
And nodded with love at each one.
Then she gazed at her man with the cowboy dream
And whispered, "Hon, it was all worth the doin'."

They laid her to rest on a hill lookin' out
On the sweep on twelve sections of range,
With a view of the house and the cattle and all
Where the wind would sing through the sage.

Her headmarker said,

> "She came West with me
> To help me to live out my dream.
> Good wife.
> Good mother.
> Good cowboy.
> Good woman.
> Can't wait to see her again."

In the open range days, and on some outfits still today, it was common for a steady hand whose health had quit him to stay on in the cow business by turning to other ranch endeavors, including taking over the cooking chores. "Old Coosie" attempts to typify those hardy western men who found it necessary to trade in their spurs for a spatula, but who still remained top hands in every way.

Old Coosie

The kid whispered 'fore the dawn, "Old Coosie's mad again.
He's talkin' to hisself like livin' is a sin.

"He's scowlin' at his sourdough and cussin' out his pots;
We may not get no breakfast the way he's goin' off."

I slid into my hightops and yawned. "Kid, now don't you fret.
He gets like that from time to time but we ain't gone hungry yet."

"I don't know," the kid replied. "His eyes are lookin' grim.
I seen 'em by the fire light and they're icy 'round the rims."

"Now listen, kid. It'll be ok. He starts out like this some morns
When he thinks back on his ridin' days. It puts him in a storm

"Knowin' he's too stiff to ride an' drag 'em to the fire,
Or step aboard a four year-old and snap him out for hire.

"Kid, Old Coosie has more cow sense than any five of us,
But when we mount up, he'll still be here a'cleanin' dishes up.

"I've knowed that man a bunch of years. He sorta took me in
When I was green and comin' on and he taught me who I am.

"Coosie savvies cow brutes; understands 'em tail to horn.
Why, ever' cowboy thing I know, I learned from watchin' him.

"And when it comes to hosses, say, you've never seen the like;
He can read 'em like the Good Book and they sure do read him back.

"I've seen him take the wild mare's colts that no one else could fork,
And in just a couple days or so they'd be trottin' off to work.

"Kid, I'll tell you whatcha do. Go and grab yourself a cup,
And then ask him sorta casual why your rope is messin' up.

"Then ask him if there's anything a feller might could try;
He'll likely bog his head and paw but let it go on by."

"If he'll take you on like he did me, you'll have a friend fer life;
That old man can teach you things that colleges can't buy.

"Go on, kid," I nodded. "And don't let him run his bluff;
He's as salty as they come but he's a tophand right enuf."

The kid took a breath, approached the fire and tried it like I said
While I eased towards the wagon to watch what Coosie did.

He eyed the kid a minute, lookin' for the joke. But seein' none, says,
"Son, I ain't no hand, but I don't mind to check yer rope."

From where I stood a'watchin' from just beyond the fly,
I thought I saw a little spark light up in Coosie's eye.

And while I listened to their talk from outside the fire's glow,
I heard him cough and tell the kid in a voice from long ago,

"Remind me after chuck tonight and we'll set aside some time
To watch yew build a loop 'er two an' watch yew cast yer twine.

"But I won't have no silly games ner dog-blamed foolishness;
Yew wanta learn then learn yew will, but I'll expect yore best."

I had known that my old friend could not refuse the kid;
He'd done the same for me one time and would do the same again.

But this time it was diff'rent as to who was helpin' who;
The kid would surenuf learn to rope, but it was good for Coosie, too.

'Course he went on with his growlin', but I could tell it was fer show
When he took a little extra care while punchin' out his dough.

By the time we caught our ponies and the sun was drawin' nigh,
Old Coosie was a whistlin' some old tune from days gone by,

And the fodder that he built that morn was good enough for swells,
With biscuits fine, taters crisp, and bacon done so well.

After chuck, the boss gave out our orders for the day;
Huntin' up the slicks that in the Spring had got away.

The kid was partnered up with me as we left camp at a trot,
And as we rode out on the day I offered one more thought:

"Remember, kid, it's no small thing to show a man respect.
It's a common word, but mighty strong, and you've done seen its effect.

"And just you pray that when you're old and runnin' low on hope,
Some kid will come and ask you if you'd help him with his rope."

I have bent my back under just enough horses to know that shoeing is one chore I really do not care to master. Besides, when our farrier comes by to tack some iron on our little remuda, he brings with him great stories as well as all the local news, including this little tale.

Ode to the Farrier

The telephone rings in the dark a.m. of a cold and wintry dawn.
The farrier groans, then picks it up while stiflin' back a yawn.
A voice comes on. "This here is Ed. My geldin's thrown a shoe.
He's all I've got that's fit to ride and I've got work to do."

Rubbin' sleep out from his eyes, he stumbles out of bed
And gallops through the shower to clear his weary head.
He builds a pot of coffee and grabs some day-old cake,
Checks his schedule and his calls for sortin' out the day.

Then he dons his Carharrt's, tops off his coffee jug
And stumbles to the pick-up midst icy wind and mud.
His vintage truck ain't pretty but she cranks up ever' time,
So half asleep, he hits the gas and points 'er out the drive.

"Let's see," he sighs. "Ed's geldin' likes to kick just for the fun,
  And if this trip's like the one's before he'll still be on the run,
Which means I'll have to help Ed catch that dirty so-and-so,
And then he'll have the nerve to ask why do I work so slow."

  Just as thought, when he arrives the geldin's on the loose.
  Dang you, Ed!, the shoer thinks, *Why can't you shake a loop?*
  And in the empty early light the geldin' wants to play,
So it's nearly eight o'clock before he's brought to bay.

  Once the horse is captured the shoer aprons up,
  Grabs his tools in frigid hands and moves in from the front.
  The geldin' casts an evil glance as the shoer taps his hock,
Selectin' height and distance for the perfect kickin' spot.

  The shoer cleans and nips and files and tries the iron for fit,
  Watchin' Geldin' formulate his plans to score a hit.
  But as he starts to nail him up, Ol' Ed speaks up and says,
"It shore is cold. I may just turn him out and work inside instead."

  The shoer breathes a silent groan while he finishes the clinch,
  Then slowly straightens out his back and rubs his frozen mitts.
  'Tis now the geldin' makes his move! He rises to his task!
His nice new shoe homes in and on the seat ... of Ol' Ed's pants!

  Now Ed, he ain't expected this. It's caught him on the sly.
  He cowboys up and even tries to chuckle in reply,
  But you can bet that more than pride's been injured in his jeans,
And you can tell Ol' Ed may just be standin' up till Spring.

  Of course ner laugh nor grin escapes the shoer's mouth;
  Just, "Here now Ed, you take a break. He's done. I'll turn him out."
  But as Ed removes his wallet, movin' gingerly and slow,
The farrier smiles. "No charge, Ed. Your horse just paid in full."

> *Those who have ridden the big circles and trails that can't be seen from the road have a sense of the long-ago times that sometimes seem to be waiting just around the bend or over the next ridge.*
>
> *And they know that if they listen carefully, the trails may softly speak of lives and times that once were.*

The Trail

The western trails know secret tales
Of those who've passed along
In the days of old, in the days of gold,
In the days of horse and gun.

> Few listen now. We've forgotten how
> As we drive our highway race
> To leave the signs and the roads behind
> And seek the slower pace.

But the trail will share with those who care
The deeds of yesteryear,
So listen well and feel the spell
As she *whispers* to your ear -

70

The land was dry and the dust was high
That Fall of Eighty-Two,
When hooves did pound across the ground
And a horse came into view.

> Atop the steed, in blood-stained jeans
> Sat a rider pale and limp.
> His side was red from where he'd bled,
> From a bullet in his hip.

With haunted eyes he looked behind
And checked his rearward trail
For sight or sound of the posse bound
To carry him to jail.

> When no one came, he groaned in pain
> And slid off to the ground.
> With reins in hand his horse and him
> Limped o'er without a sound

To a rocky ledge at the trail's edge
Where he dropped the saddlebags
That held the gold that he had stole,
And that got him shot to rags.

> Through eyes now dim he looked again
> But no riders did he see,
> So he buckled down there on the ground
> And rested on his knees.

With stifled moan he moved a stone,
Then dug with fingers raw
Below its base to make a place
For the gold his blood had bought.

He dug it deep to hide his keep,
Covered it with sand,
Rolled back the stone with another moan,
Then forced himself to stand.

> The stone replaced, the horseman faced
> His mount and willed his feet
> To crawl aboard and set him o'er
> Upon his weary seat.

With ner a word he touched his spurs
And disappeared from view,
Leaving behind as his only sign
That stone that he had moved.

> And no one knows about the gold
> These hundred years and more,
> For the outlaw died upon his ride
> From that bullet that he bore.

With loss of blood, he tumbled from
His mount and rolled far down
Off the trail in a shaded swale,
His body never found.

> The posse came but looked in vain
> For outlaw, mount, and gold;
> They galloped past and missed their chance
> To hear what the trail could've told.

Oh, they said they tried to make the find,
That they checked the trail with care.
But after all, their homes did call
And they'd done their duty square.

The posse failed to ask the trail,
The trail that might have told
About the gold and the guardian stone
And the outlaw dead and cold.

So there it lays to this very day,
The gold beneath the ground.
And no one knows, for sure not those
Who speed by elsewhere bound.

Yes, the western trails know secret tales
Of those who've passed along
In the days of old, in the days of gold,
In the days of horse and gun.

Can you hear the trail *whisper*
The tales that might be told?
Of early days and of western ways?
Of an outlaw?
And his gold?

*The western lifestyle,
with its fluctuating
prices, unpredictable
weather, and the ever-
rising cost of simply
staying in business, just
naturally calls for a
spirit of optimism. This
rhyme offers a light-
hearted example of that
spirit.*

Lost An' Found

Down to the local Co-op store, hangin' there inside the door
They've placed a poster board where folks apply
Notices of work fer hire and things fer sale to sure admire,
But the Lost An' Found's what really caught my eye.

On a scrap of paper neat, pinned to the board fer all to see
I read the loss of someone's fav'rite pet.
Now pedigree was not the theme, just ways to recognize id seen,
And this is how the little notice went.

"Wanted back, a dog we lost. Reward is offered – name the cost;
We'll do what's right to have him home again.
He's a friendly sorta dog you see, and a member of the family;
To lose him now would be most like a sin.

He's black and tan except fer where a dose of mange removed his hair,
And a coyote got one ear three weeks ago.
He's scarred up some from doin' battle with the neighbor's proddy cattle,
And while he's game, it's left him kinder slow.

You'll note a lump there on his chin from where Ol' Muley cow-kicked him;
It left him with a few less teeth to chew.
His rear-end's bowed and kinder swayed; I backed the tractor where he lay
And it dented up a vertebra or two.

The poor Ol' guy done lost a leg whilst playin' with the hayin' rig,
But he tries real hard to act like it don't show.
He's only got one eye to gawk – lost the other to a rock
Some lamebrain kid threw at him years ago,

But even with the wrecks he's had, we want him back an' awful bad;
He's a dandy and a pard and mighty plucky.
He won't be hard to recognize, so call him in if he is spied;
He answers mostly to the name of . . . 'Lucky' . . ."

> *I count it a blessing to have looked at some mighty pretty mountain country while in the company of the subject of this poem. He is missed, and I'm sorry he's gone.*

Goodbye Ol' Pard *(for Tony)*

It's hard to say goodbye ol' pard, after all the camps we've shared.
You've been true blue along the trail and you'll be missed for sure.

I'll think about the times we've had while travelin' side by side,
The mountain trails and ranges crossed as we've both made our ride.

I guess I never told you, pard, but you knew cows the best
Of any pal I ever had across this cowboy west.

Now I'm not one for fancy words, but I need to let you know
You've been a surenuf friend to me a'goin' down the road.

You know well that I don't run to words all flowered up,
But I'd like to thank you kindly for the times you listened up

To what I had to say when we were out there on the range,
Workin' mountain country or punchin' in the sage.

76

Pard, you never tried to judge me but you took me as I was,
And I hope I done the same for you the way a pardner should.

It's mighty hard to see you go, although I know it's time
For you to strike the homeward trail and cross that last divide.

I hope your trail is easy and your way marked fresh and clear
By other pards who've gone before to welcome you up there.

I shall be forever grateful to count you as my friend,
Although I know there's many folks who would not understand

How man and beast could be so close; how a cowboy and his dog
Could call each other *friend*. Happy trails, ol' pard. So long.

This bit of silliness was birthed after I finished reading a little magazine article about modern ranching methods in, of all places, Japan, where it seems even the cow work is performed via technology. Well, whatever works I guess . . .

The Modern Rancher

The monthly *Stockman's Journal* fairly bulges with the news
Of modern means to manage cows and increase profits, too.
Its pages share the latest trends on how to calve, and when,
And where to brand and by what means when markin' critter skins.

Contained therein you'll find some words I surely can't pronounce,
Describin' feed and supplements to give your cows more b-o-u-n-c-e,
Not to mention scientific terms tossed in to note
The latest threat to the health of the bovines that you own.

But this aside, the latest trend I read the other day
Sorta makes me scratch my head to see things get this way;
It seems the *modern* rancher now trails his cows to feed
By pickin' up a telephone and givin' them a ***beep***

On gadgetry electric he has slung around their heads,
And they come in to see just what their beeper message said!
I s'pose it works and works right well, this callin' on the phone,
But what's the modern rancher do if he gets a *busy* tone?

> *We all hold dear to our hearts the stereotypical image of the great American cowboy, with his (or her) jeans, boots and, perhaps most importantly, hat. But does the hat make the cowboy, or does the cowboy make the hat?*

Real Cowboys

I was ridin' back from town and packin' precious mail
For the crew we had back at the ranch and still out on the trail.
I was settin' nice and easy in my old and trusted kack,
Ridin' Mike t'wards a gate we used for town and back.

But about the time I touched the reins to point Mike for the gate,
I hears the honkin' of a horn from off the interstate.
I glanced up sorta casual to see what could it be,
And there my eyes beheld a family, wavin' straight at *me!*

There's a feller, wife, and kid all standin' by this van,
Each grinnin' big and pointin' with their attention on *this* hand.
I figured maybe they was lost and I might point their way,
But then as me and Mike gets close I hears the weaner say,

"Do you think he is, Dad? A real cowboy? He's wearin' jingly spurs.
His jeans are tucked down in his boots like in the cowboy shows.
He's got on chaps and see that rope hanging on his horn?
And there's his vest and silky scarf just like I read they own."

I must confess the kiddo's talk went straight up to my head;
I sat a little straighter in the saddle as we neared.
I tweaked on my old moustache to set it square and true;
I figured they might even want a picture 'fore they'uz through.

Now I allowed the kid was right – I was cowboy, that's for shore,
From hightop boots that grazed my knees to the dusty shirt I wore.
If these tourist-types were on the scout for a *real* tophand to see,
I had the answer to their prayers, and the answer, pard, was **me**!

I they was wantin' cowboy, they'd found the right galoot;
I'd cut my teeth on bovine types and I'd taught the owl to hoot.
Why truth be known I'd done it all at least a time or two
So when it came to cowboys, I'd be the one to choose.

Well, we saunters up. I builds a smile. I doffs my feedstore cap.
(The day bein' kinder windy, my felt was at the ranch.)
Their grins all fell. Dad said, "Get in. I can't believe we stopped for that."
And he added as they drove away, "Real cowboys wear cowboy hats."

Born To Cowboy

There's somethin' about a cowcamp night that sets a body thinkin'
As you lay there in your soogans warm and tired.
With the fire reduced to glowin' and the night breeze gently blowin',
You'll find yourself reflectin' on your life.

You'll catch yourself considerin' all that's gone before;
The camps and friends your trail has took you to;
The bad ones that you rode and the times that you've been throwed,
And how you felt when cowology was new.

All in all it ain't been bad the way you've spent the years,
Doin' what so many only dream;
Livin' with the land and tryin' to make a hand,
Bein' what God intended you to be.

You'll think about your cowboy dreams when first you heard the call,
Knowin' you was born for horse and range;
The spread that you would own and the ranch you'd call your own,
With a mate who would take and keep your name.

There was that gal from middle school - the one you had your eye on?
You had it planned to someday tie the knot,
But plans don't always matter when a girl is gettin' older
And she got tired of waitin' and moved on.

It looked so plain and simple when you were young and sure;
Just dab a loop on all that you would hold.
Do the work and make a hand and keep your honest name,
And save your pay for all you'd someday own.

Now, layin' here and gazin' at the stars way overhead,
You know that Life don't make succeedin' quite that easy.
O' you had the try and your dream was good and you wanted it to be,
But the passin' of the seasons took their dallies on your dream.

And then you'll get to missin' the folks you left back home;
Your Ma who cried when you said goodbye.
And Pa, who understood and said, "Son, now be a man,
And pen a note to Mama by and by."

So you'll wonder if it's selfishness that causes you to stay,
To ride for beef and beans in heat and cold.
You'll wonder if way down inside you're only still a kid,
Just playin' at your life while growin' old.

But reflectin' on the sunsets and the mornin's that you've known,
The horses rode across the rangeland sea,
The campfire coffee and nights like these,
You know that *cowboy* is what you were surely born to be.

I got the idea for "The Dead Cow Story" from a cowboy who says he doesn't even remember telling me the tale. But since I wrote it, there have been quite a few folks who have allowed that they, or someone they know, have had a similar experience.

The Dead Cow Story

RD and me was partnered up.
'Twas Spring and the season of calves.
We'uz edgin' a draw dumpin' into Dry Crick
When we spied this young heifer laid out.

As we circled around and rode up from behind,
She just laid there like she was in bed.
Her ears didn't flick and her ribs didn't rise
And both of us knowed she was dead.

Then RD detected two frail little legs
Stickin' out from under her tail.
Inside of that heifer was a calf wantin' born
And he surenuf needed to bail!

We couldn't ride off - twern't the cowboy way;
That baby was needful of us
To figger a way to help him get out
Before his future went bust.

We knew we had to get to him quick and
Dab a rope 'round his toes.
Then we'ud pull him to sunshine and safety and air
And give him his chance for to grow.

RD dismounted to handle the chore
Of savin' the poor little thing.
I held his pony while he built him a loop
And threw a good hitch 'round them feet.

Then slick as a cowboy can make tracks for town,
He sat down behind of that cow.
He planted his feet astride of her tail
And pulled back just like he knew how.

Now I will allow we were somewhat surprised
When that heifer jumped straight back to life!
She'd only been restin' while havin' her babe
And had woke with that yank on the line!

That bovine took off like she was late for a date
And she shore was packin' the mail,
With RD's wrist caught up in his rope
And him just aft of her tail.

Now RD just hates to work from the ground,
And he'ud rather go hungry than walk,
But that rope was dallied around of his wrist
So he figgered that maybe he'd like to keep up.

Well, they both quit the country with the cow in the lead
And RD a'runnin' the drags.
That rope was stretched out like a shot from a gun,
With my pardner boundin' in twenty foot strides.

It made quite a scene as they busted the sage,
And RD was keepin' up slick.
But that heifer was startin' to hit her own stride
As they came to the edge of Dry Crick.

One should not be misled by the name of that stream,
'Cause snowmelt in March can run high.
That cow skipped across on cloven-web feet
While RD sorta ski'ed right behind.

'Course RD is tryin' each step of the race
To get himself shut of his string,
But whenever he managed to grab him some slack
The heifer would pour on the speed.

'Course I'uz sure tryin' to rescue my pard
From this heifer of biblical fame,
But whenever I closed she'd turn straight away
And off they would lope once again.

We soon drew abreast of this new five-strand fence,
But that bovine never slackened her pace.
She bellied on over - RD took a leap -
And cleared the **fourth** strand with Olympian grace.

Next thing they hit was a pocket of brush,
Mostly Catclaw with thorns big as nails.
RD was gettin' this look on his face
Like his luck was beginnin' to fail.

She towed 'im on through an' then out the far side,
Leavin' most of his cloes in the brush.
He was startin' to show the effects of this bout
And looked like he'd had near unuf.

I guess you might say he was some worse fer wear,
With his shirt ripped clear off his back.
He'uz muddy and wet from ski'in' the crick
And that fence and the briars hadn't cut him no slack.

But along about then the cow slowed fer air;
RD took aholt of his line
In his bare teeth and chewed and gnawed back and forth
Till them strands began to unwind.

Whilst RD was eatin', I got me a loop
Throwed around of the heifer's young neck,
Then taken some dallies around of the horn
And backed up and stretched her out neat.

RD finally managed to gnaw through the rope.
(Had to since he'd misplaced his knife.)
His wrist was purple and as big as a log
And his mouth was drippin' with Rope Strand Delight.

As we all took a break the calf finally came,
A dandy to make his mom proud.
Rd just sighed and looked at his wrist
And then glanced up at me and allowed -

"Pardner, I've cowboyed for pay since I was a kid.
I grew up on tales of the range,
And I've heard me some stories to make a man cringe
'Bout cowboys and cowboy ways.

I've been in some wrecks where I figgered to die,
But nothin' comes close to today.
And if **ever** I chance on another dead cow,
I'm gonna shoot her and then just ride away!

Many of us tend to look back to the way things used to be, and allow our wishful perceptions of history to color the old days with a mighty handsome brush. Personally, I think that's a pretty good thing, as long as we don't forget to be thankful for our todays and tomorrows, too. If you are one of those folks who was born "a hundred years too late", this poem is for you.

When Once I Was Young
and a Cowboy

When once I was young and a cowboy,
All the ranges were open and free,
And the wind comin' down
Made a siren sound
That beckoned and tugged at my dreams.

When once I was young and a cowboy,
All the stars in the sky did I own.
All the hills and the plains
Of the far cattle range –
They were mine wherever I rode.

When I was young, how my pony did run
As we followed the wild bovine.
It was ropes pullin' tight and the campfire at night;
It was saddles
And it was spurs and it was life.

When once I was young and a cowboy,
'Fore the fences divided the land,
Then I owned all I saw,
All the ridges and the draws,
When I rode for the pride of the brand.

When once I was young and a cowboy,
How I thrilled for to answer the call
Of the trail reachin' long,
Of the night-herdin' song,
Of the dust, and the buck, and the bawl.

O', when I was young, how my pony did run
As we followed the wild bovine.
It was ropes pullin' tight and the campfire at night
And it was saddles
And it was spurs and it was life.

But now it's all gone and there's only a song
To remember the life that we lived
When the ranges were free
For young cowboys like me;
Now I'm old, but I'm glad that I lived when I did,

When once I was young and a cowboy.

> *I sure do admire riding back in at the end of a good day. There's something pretty special about turning your four-legged pardner out for a good roll and some oats, and settling yourself in for the night. Yep, "day's end" is a real special time around our place.*

Day's End

Lord, it's time we shut the gate on yet another day.
 I've grained the horses an' brushed 'em down
  An' turned 'em out with hay.

I've ate my chuck and read awhile and drank my final cup;
 All the crew is sleepin' now
  While I'm laid here my bunk,

An' I just been a'thinkin' 'bout today an' all we done;
 Rode a lot of miles you bet,
  An' worked from sun to sun.

92

I'uz glad to ketch that one ol' cow;
 You know the one I mean?
  She's bested us the summer long, all the boys an' me.

Did You see on Bugle Ridge today, that coyote sittin' there?
 He looked like he might own the world
  An' him without a care.

An' did You hear that flock of geese a'wingin' overhead?
 Flyin' South to Mexico
  To winter there, I guess.

Lord, the thought occurs to me that I am kindly blessed
 To live out here where You're the Boss
  Of all of Life's events;

Of newborn calves, an' mornin' sun, an' Quakie leaves in Fall;
 Of Winter snow, an' cowcamp,
  An' the bull elks' eerie call.

Not many folks have got to do the things I've been allowed,
 Like today me takin' dallies
  On that mossy-horned ol' cow,

Or sittin' round the fire at noon before we headed out
 To check that brush along the crick
  For strays a'hangin' out.

I surenuf do appreciate livin' like I do,
 Viewin' Life from horseback;
  Why, I'm one of just a few

That gets to do for wages what most can only dream,
 Livin' in their cities,
  Only cowboyin' in their dreams.

O', I know we all have got our special jobs to work,
 Be it bankin', sales, or teachin'
  Or nursin' those who hurt,

But I'm proud You signed me on for the western way of life.
 Well, that's all that I was thinkin' Lord,
  An' it's gettin' late -

                    Good night.

This final piece began life in a motel room in Elko, Nevada when we were out there for the annual poetry and music gather a while back.

The initial seed for the poem was sown with the passing comment a friend made while we were out to supper one evening. He mentioned the word "medusa" in a story he was telling us (the Medusa was an evil goddess of ancient mythology) and when that single word started galloping around inside my head, I just couldn't shake it.

By the time my bride and I started back for Wyoming, I was already scribbling lines as fast as I could and so I'm afraid she got stuck handling the driving chores most of the way, bless her heart.

Well, the idea that came from that one casual word quickly took on a life of its own as "The Medusa Mare" stretched out across the paper at a high lope. She simply would not respond to the reins and I finally had no choice but to give her her head until she decided we were through.

I hope you enjoy the reading as much as I did the writing.

The Medusa Mare

This story has its end
Beneath a narrow, rocky path
    Which cut its ancient, clinging way
    Above a gathered mass

Of barren, silent boulders
Brooding in the wind,
    Thrown down in timeless ages past
    As if by Satan's hand.

Now if a rider on the path
Will steal a glance below,
        He'll likely see on one gray stone
        A smear of sorrel gold, but

Beginnings precede endings,
And so this tale should start
        With my Annie. And her filly.
        And the love in Annie's heart.

My Annie girl and I were wed
When she was but eighteen,
        Offering her hand to me,
        A cowboy young and lean.

To make a home, I took a job
Up on the summer range,
        For there we'd have a cabin snug
        To share our marriage dreams.

And it was grand! So grand
Mere words can ne'er express
        Remembrance of those sunny days
        And nights of happiness,

For I was just for Annie
And she was just for me,
        With not one soul to interrupt
        Or spoil our youthful dreams.

Then came Molly.
Annie found her 'mongst a stand
        Of aspen bordering the stream
        That near our cabin ran.

Annie'd heard a plaintive nicker
And walked back in to find
      A frightened weanling filly
      Pawing at the side

Of the cold and stiff remains
Of a gaunted, toothless mare,
      Reduced to fodder for the wolves,
      Beyond the point of care.

"Annie'd heard a plaintive nicker . . ."

Annie guessed a catamount
Had tried to down her foal
      And that she had purchased life with death,
      Paying with her own.

So Annie coaxed the filly home
And placed her in the pen
      Where they together spent the day
      'Til later I rode in.

Tho' to my shame, I must confess
That I did not like her there,
      Stealing Annie's laugh and touch
      That only I should share.

O' the filly was a pretty thing;
Her color sorrel-gold
      With flaxen mane and tail to match,
      Her carriage proud and bold.

Her legs were muscled long and deep;
They hinted at the speed
      That someday would be hers to use
      To race against the breeze.

'Twas clear to see right from the start
That Annie'd made a friend.
      She would stroke and hug the filly's neck
      Then stroke her yet again

And speak to her in gentle tones
And breathe into her nose;
      'Molly", Annie called her,
      And told her she was home.

But I beheld a certain look
Behind the filly's eyes;
     While they offered love to Annie,
     They showed me black despise.

At first I thought the violent death
That quick had claimed her dam
     Had prompted her to recognize
     My Annie as a friend

And that she would, in time,
Accept me by her side.
     But as the summer spent itself
     I found she'd not abide

My presence, hand, or voice
If Annie were not there,
     Nor would she deign to glance my way
     Except with baleful glare.

O' I tried to show me friendly;
I swear I truly did!
     But her response was just that look
     That showed she wished me dead.

I finally concluded
That while Annie was her friend,
     The filly hated anyone
Who t'ween the two might stand.

And she was smart,
And quick enough to learn
     To shoulder me or try a bite
     When Annie's back was turned.

Or she'd swing that pretty head at me
And push me hard away,
      Then act as though t'were nothing
      But a growing child at play.

I knew she'd fooled my Annie
And that Annie didn't see
      The hate that Molly held inside,
      Reserved in full for me.

So, though Annie never heard it used,
I changed the filly's name –
      I christened her *Medusa*
      Of ancient, evil fame.

As that summer reached its end,
We headed down below
      To townwork through the winter,
      Away from mountain snows.

Of course my Annie's filly
Made the trip as well,
      And used those lazy winter days
      To build upon the spell

That she had cast on Annie,
Where Annie saw no wrong;
      Just could not see that look behind
      Her eyes of jealous brown.

But as for me? The look was clear;
She hated me so deep
      That she'd have liked to kill me
      If Annie had not seen.

'Twas sure they made a pretty pair,
My Annie and her friend.
    The townfolk thought them handsome
    As round the town they went,

With Molly close to Annie,
And no rope to make it so;
    It seemed I was the only one
    Who was marked to be her foe.

"Twas sure they made a pretty pair ..."

* * * * * * * * * *

And so it went.
Five years flew swiftly by;
    High-up range in summer,
    Then town for winter's bite.

Medusa grew into a mare,
A beauty to behold;
    Annie rode her everywhere
    With just a bareback hold.

"'Twas almost like that nursery rhyme
Handed down of old;
    'Everywhere that Annie went
    The mare was sure to go.'"

The two were close like sisters,
Although you'll think me strange,
    But had you chanced to see them
    You'd know how true that rang.

And the hate Medusa held for me,
Carried deep within?
    Had shown itself in misses near
    When she'd tried to do me in.

For awhile I'd vainly tried
To win her fledgling trust,
    But I had finally given up
    And rather learned to watch

For yet another evil plan
To spring forth from her breast –
    A kick at flies imagined
    That barely missed my chest;

"I learned to watch for yet another evil plan . . ."

The shove against the fence rail
That almost crushed me there;
    The head that nearly broke my jaw
    When swung with deadly care.

Why did I not destroy her?
You ask, and rightly so.
    I'd have shot her with a smile!
    But then Annie would have known,

And I could not hurt my Annie
Nor crease her face with care,
    For she saw not the hate that burned
    In her medusa mare.

All tales must have an ending
And so it is with mine.
    It was August on the summer range
    And once again was I

Employed to watch the cattle there.
Our cabin was the same
    That we had known in youthful bliss
    When Annie took my name.

The medusa mare was there of course,
Or 'Molly' if preferred,
    Still an angel to my Annie,
    Though to me a Lucifer.

By now I'd learned her evil ways
And would leave her well alone
    To spend her time with Annie
    When I was out from home.

Then came the raging fever
That struck my Annie down.
    It left her hot and limp,
    Unable to rebound.

I tried all homespun remedies
That ever I had known
    But Annie only weakened
    With each breath and weary groan.

I knew that quick I had to find
A doctor for my love,
    Or she was soon to join the host
    Of angels up above.

But we were in the mountains,
While help was far below;
        I'd take my horse and make the run
        To bring the doctor home.

I kissed my love and squeezed her hand,
Then turned away to go
        When out the door there came a *c-r-a-c-k*
        From lightning-studded storm!

The lightning struck not far away;
It singed and burnt the air!
        The horses bolted through the fence
        And disappeared in fear!

All except for one. That stood.
And looked me in the eye;
        The mare I called Medusa,
        The mare that oft had tried

To strike me down and kill me
To make me dearly pay
        For daring to love Annie
        And for taking her away.

But now I had to trust the mare;
There was no other choice.
        So I offered her my saddle
        And I spoke with urgent voice

That we both stood to lose our love;
That Annie would not survive
        Unless we called a truce
        And brought a doctor to her side.

"So I offered her my saddle and I spoke with urgent voice . . ."

And so . . . she let me ride her.
Into the storm we sped,
        Along, around, across and down,
        I gave the mare her head.

She took that narrow rocky path
With no slack'ning to her pace
        And galloped off the mountain
        To seek a doctor's grace.

That evil mare Medusa
Raced before the storm,
        Raced all through the slashing night
        To bring us down below

Where quick I found the doctor
Who said that he would come,
      And quickly turned we up the trail
      To make the run again.

"She took that narrow rocky path with no slack'ning to her pace . . ."

The mare I called Medusa
Was drenched in sweated foam.
      Although she never slackened,
      Her labored breathing groaned

As up we fled toward the one
Whose love we both held dear.
      Medusa never faltered
       'Til that narrow path we neared.

I urged her o'er without a thought
For what might lie below,
      My only need to reach the side
       Of Annie lying low.

'Twas then Medusa stumbled, and
O', how she scrambled to regain!
      But muscles that had run the night
       Could not respond in time!

I vaulted from the saddle
But held on to the reins;
      I tried to pull her 'ere she fell –
       Alas . . . my pulls were vain.

Down. And down. And down she fell
To dash the rocks below.
      Ne'er a sound she offered,
       But as I watched her go

She fixed me with those eyes of hers,
Those eyes of fiery hate.
      But rather than the look of old,
       I saw the fires replaced

With eyes of understanding;
Somehow she'd come to know
      That I was *not* her enemy
       And had never wished it so.

"I tried to pull her 'ere she fell . . ."

Now, with no means left to speed my way
I waved the doctor on,
      Gasping vague directions
      To send him on alone.

I trudged behind, my heart gone cold,
A numbness in my soul.
      Time lost all its meaning
      'Til I faced our cabin door.

The doctor's horse was standing by
With head low near the ground.
      The doctor must be then inside.
      Too late? What had he found?

With fearful tread I entered in,
Breathing prayers the while
      That Annie had *not* left me,
      But that I'd see her smile.

"With fearful tread I entered in, breathing prayers the while . . ."

The doctor had arrived in time!
By Annie's side he stood
      And nodded. Her recovery would be slow
      But her recovery would be good.

111

I took my place beside her bed
And held her hand in mine
  And kissed it with my thankful tears
  To God that she'd survive.

The doctor stayed throughout the night
And watched the fever ebb.
  "'Tis only speed and Heaven's grace
  That pulled her through," he said.

"An hour more and she'd have died,
But now rest will serve her well;
  You must wait awhile to tell her
  Of how her Molly fell.

"The news would surely break her heart
And we can't afford the chance
  Until her health can bear it;
  I do not envy you that task, for

"The bond they shared was known to all.
I am sure you realize
  That Molly's run is due the thanks
  For saving Annie's life."

With dawn the doctor parted
To take the trail back down,
  Leaving Annie to my care
  And the healing rest she'd found.

And of the weeks that followed
There is but naught to say.
  Annie gained her strength the while
  'Til came that dreaded day;

"Let me sit outside," she said,
"Where I may smell the pines.
　　　And bring to me my Molly girl
　　　That I might stroke her side."

I waited for a moment,
Seeking words to tell;
　　　To tell her the Medusa Mare
　　　Lay broken 'neath the trail,

For I had lacked the courage
To speak her fate before,
　　　To break the news the mare had died
　　　To bring the doctor o'er.

"My love," I finally answered,
"Although I hardly can,
　　　There's something I must tell you
　　　And I'll hope you understand."

And so I shared our hellish ride
That night against the storm,
　　　And told her of our frighted run
　　　To reach the cabin door.

Then, "Annie, it was your Molly
Who led the doctor home,
　　　But it was she who fell to strike
　　　The boulders far below.

"Annie, dear Annie, your Molly horse
Gave her all that night,
　　　And ne'er shall I forget her,
　　　Nor how she made the ride."

And so this story ends
Beneath a narrow rocky path
  That cuts its ancient clinging way
  Above a gathered mass

Of barren, silent boulders
Brooding in the wind,
  Thrown down in timeless ages past
  As if by Satan's hand.

And if a rider on the path
Will steal a glance below,
  He'll likely see on one gray stone
  A smear . . . of sorrel gold.

And he may look and wonder
Of what is lying there.
  But I will know. It is *Molly*,
    For there is no *Medusa Mare*.

114